STAR WARS™

A-WING

THRUST VECTOR CONTROL
LASER CANNON
NOVALDEX SUBLIGHT ENGINES (2)
CONCUSSION MISSILE LAUNCHER

STAR WARS™
A-WING

INSIDE THE RESISTANCE'S
HIGH-SPEED INTERCEPTOR

WRITTEN BY MICHAEL KOGGE

INCREDI
BUILDS™

a division of
INSIGHT EDITIONS
San Rafael, California

INTRODUCTION

In starfighter combat, the slightest advantage in speed or maneuverability can mean the difference between life and death. An extra boost of thrust can place an enemy vessel in the crosshairs a moment before the craft's pilot can trigger its weapon systems. Likewise, the more nimble the craft, the more able it is to avoid a crippling laser barrage. With these variables in mind, Rebel Alliance engineers set out to produce the fastest, most maneuverable starfighter they could—and the A-wing interceptor was born.

Shaped like a wedge, with a knife-like prow that cuts through the stormiest atmospheres, the A-wing originated from a Clone Wars-era starfighter, the Delta-7 *Aethersprite*. Shortly after the end of the Clone Wars, Kuat Systems Engineering improved upon its Delta-7 design to develop an R-22 prototype that tested the limits of speed and maneuverability. Though the newly established Galactic Empire did not approve the company mass-producing the R-22, Tammuz-an royalty purchased the batch of prototypes for their planetary defense fleet, calling them "Spearheads" because of their resemblance to a ceremonial Tammuz-an spear.

More than a decade later, during the early days of the Galactic Civil War, several rebel cells procured a number of the Tammuz-an Spearheads and found that they were highly customizable. A network of rebel mechanics, who nicknamed themselves the "Underground Engineers," retooled the fighter with whatever parts were accessible and rigged up a grease monkey's dream. They updated the weapons, installed new tech, and swapped the original engines for a pair of Novaldex J-77s, the fastest available. The durable Spearhead frame had the strength to carry these giant sublight engines without buckling under their torque, yet it was remarkably lightweight, offering pilots a level of manual control comparable to that available in Sienar Fleet Systems's TIE fighters. These modifications made the craft, dubbed the A-wing, the swiftest starfighter in the rebel fleet and a more-than-worthy match for the Empire's interceptors.

Detractors carp that the A-wing is nothing other than two engines strapped to a cockpit. Though that is, in essence, true, an adept pilot can execute daring stunts and maneuvers in an A-wing that the more rugged X-wing or heavily armed Y-wing cannot. Its success is corroborated by the longevity of its military service. Decades after the Rebel Alliance first deployed the A-wing, an upgraded model remains in active use in the Resistance fleet. The fighter retains its preeminence in speed and maneuverability and continues to give the Resistance pilots an edge against First Order TIEs.

RZ-2 A-WING

When upgrading the original A-wing starfighter after the war with the Empire, engineers stuck to its sleek original design and managed to juice even more thrust from its massive engines. Few starfighters come close to challenging the A-wing's speed in either space or atmospheric flight.

TECHNICAL SPECIFICATIONS

MANUFACTURER: Kuat Systems Engineering

MODEL: RZ-2 A-wing

CLASS: Starfighter

WIDTH/HEIGHT/DEPTH: 4.623 m × 2.016 m × 7.682 m

WEAPONRY: Two laser cannons; two concussion missile launchers

SHIELDS: Yes

MAXIMUM SPEED: 5,200 G (space) / 1,350 kph (atmosphere)

HYPERDRIVE: Class 1

LIFE SUPPORT SYSTEMS: Yes

CREW: 1

CONSUMABLES: One-week supply

COST: 190,000 New Republic credits new; 115,000 used (military requisition charges)

RESISTANCE RESERVE

The New Republic cut production of RZ-2 A-wings to a minimum during its demilitarization efforts. Nevertheless, the Resistance managed to acquire some of the craft to bolster its tiny fleet. These starfighters now protect the Resistance's capital ships and assault bombers.

FABRITECH ANS-9E FORWARD SENSOR: Gathers and feeds raw data about surrounding craft and objects into the flight computer and targeting system. Includes 78-o4 arrays for broad scans of potential enemies.

INCOM GBK-885 HYPERDRIVE MOTIVATORS (2): Installed in each engine nacelle, creating a double circuit to initiate jumps to lightspeed.

CARGO COMPARTMENT: Small space under the cockpit stores survival gear and consumables.

HULL: Lightweight durasteel plates cover a titanium alloy frame.

TARGETING SENSORS (2): Attached above laser cannons to improve aim.

STABILIZER WINGS (2): Vertical, movable vanes help control flight, particularly in atmosphere.

THRUSTER VECTOR CONTROLS (2): Make microsecond adjustments to thrust for maneuverability.

RSEIK HULLSPACE F2E "ENERGY ARMOR" DEFLECTOR SHIELD GENERATOR: Located behind the cockpit, the generator uses excess energy from the engines to project a bubble around the craft.

COCKPIT: State-of-the-art flight systems feature a Microaxial LpL-849 flight controller and a Pallas "Crosshairs" 98j precision holo-targeter.

IRILLIAD "BLINDER" 4B2 JAMMING ARRAY: Broadcasts data bursts to disrupt enemy sensors.

ZIJA GO-4 LASER CANNONS (2): Swivel in a 120-degree vertical range.

THRUSTER CONTROL JETS (2): Supply added performance boost to sublights.

DYMEK HM-22 CONCUSSION MISSILE LAUNCHERS (2): Each loaded with a six-missile magazine.

NOVALDEX K-88 "EVENT HORIZON" SUBLIGHT ENGINES (2): Two enormous Klyd-Marro 67e fusion cores, fueled by cryogenic power tubes, provide the massive thrust to achieve high speeds.

SWIFT STRIKER

When time is of the essence, Resistance naval commanders turn to the A-wing. Its ability to outrace other ships of its class helps the Resistance survive the war against the First Order.

SNEAK ATTACK

The A-wing's speed makes it ideal for "hit-and-fade" missions against enemy targets. It can slip in, unleash its lasers or launch its missiles, and then dart out—often before the other side knows what has hit them.

WATCH OUT

An A-wing doesn't need to be behind its quarry to shoot; its hail of lasers can come from above or below. This is due to its rotating cannons, which allow pilots a broader firing arc than in starfighters with fixed-position lasers.

RAPID RESPONDER

Able to reach a set of coordinates faster than any other craft, A-wings are often sent to aid friendly starfighters under attack. Many pilots owe their lives to an A-wing's sudden intervention.

A-WING SLASH

A strategy known as the "A-wing Slash" calls for slower fighters like X-wings to engage with a group of enemies, distracting them and sowing confusion, before A-wings dive into the battle, making a devastating surprise attack.

SPACE ARROW

The A-wing's wedge-shaped chassis not only assists in atmospheric flight. At high speeds, the sharp edge of its prow can puncture dense durasteel and can become quite the deadly projectile with its explosive fuel systems. Pilots in a doomed A-wing have been known to make a final statement by flinging their damaged fighter into enemy ships.

THIN SKIN

The A-wing's incredible speed comes at a price. The streamlined craft is constructed with lighter hull alloys and weak deflectors so that it can achieve top velocities. As a result, one solid laser barrage can often be enough to overwhelm its energy shields, penetrate the hull, and destroy the fragile craft. Therefore, an A-wing pilot's survival rests almost solely on his or her ability to use the craft's unparalleled maneuverability to avoid enemy fire.

OLD PARTS, NEW BUILD

Built from miscellaneous tech and accessories, A-wings are prone to mechanical breakdown and are in constant need of maintenance to keep in good working condition.

SPACE JAM

An A-wing's avionics system retunes the electromagnetic noise created by the Novaldex engines and broadcasts wide-spectrum interference that blinds multi-spectral imagers. While larger ships with more sophisticated sensors are immune to this jamming, smaller ships like TIE fighters find it difficult to track an A-wing or even call for aid when they are in its vicinity.

ALL ALONE

The A-wing is without a droid socket, so its pilot has no astromech assistant to help with navigation or repairs. The navicomputer can be programmed for a number of hyperspace coordinates, but on-the-fly lightspeed jumps can be tricky.

RZ-1 A-WING

Often considered the Rebellion's answer to the Empire's TIE interceptor, the RZ-1 A-wing outdid its Imperial rival and was regarded as one of the fastest starfighters in the galaxy.

TECHNICAL SPECIFICATIONS

MANUFACTURER: Kuat Systems Engineering

MODEL: RZ-1 A-wing

CLASS: Starfighter

WIDTH/HEIGHT/DEPTH: 4.623 m × 2.016 m × 7.682 m

WEAPONRY: Laser cannons (2); concussion missile launchers (2)

SHIELDS: Yes

MAXIMUM SPEED: 5,100 G (space) / 1,300 kph (atmosphere)

HYPERDRIVE: Class 1

LIFE SUPPORT SYSTEMS: Yes

CREW: 1

CONSUMABLES: One-week supply

COST: 175,000 Imperial credits new; 105,000 used (military requisition charges)

BORSTEL RG-9 LASER CANNONS (2): Rotate up and down in a 120-degree range, powered by dedicated converters.

ACCESS PANEL: Allows easy repair of the most vital systems.

COCKPIT: Internal systems include IN-344-B "Sightline" holographic imager, Microaxial LpL-449 flight controller, and Fabritech ANq 3.6 targeting computer.

FABRITECH ANS-7E FORWARD SENSOR: Main data collector. Usually coupled with PG-7u short-range primary threat analysis grid and PA-94 long-range phased tachyon detection array.

DYMEK HM-6 CONCUSSION MISSILE LAUNCHERS (2): Each loaded with a six-missile magazine.

SIRPLEX Z-9 DEFLECTOR SHIELD PROJECTOR:
Projects a layer of ray shielding from prow to stern.

TRAINING JETS

Since the A-wing was so difficult to fly, the Alliance constructed a barebones training version of the ship known as the RZ-1T that pilots used to practice their maneuvers. A second seat in the cockpit accommodated a flight instructor.

HULL: Lightweight durasteel plates cover a titanium alloy frame.

MIRADYNE 4X-PHANTOM SHORT-RANGE SENSOR JAMMER: Sends interference to nearby sensors.

INCOM GBK-785 HYPERDRIVE MOTIVATORS (2): Engages both engine nacelles to make the jump to lightspeed.

NOVALDEX J-77 "EVENT HORIZON" SUBLIGHT ENGINES (2): Dual MPS Bpr-99 fusion reactors power the engines.

DELTA-7 AETHERSPRITE

In the waning days of the Old Republic, the Jedi Council commissioned a starfighter built to complement a Jedi pilot's extraordinary reflexes and skills. The result was the Delta-7 *Aethersprite*, also known as the "Jedi starfighter." Its sleek arrowhead design and its exceptional speed and agility would inspire the RZ-1 A-wing in the decades to come.

COCKPIT: Instrumentation modified specifically for Jedi pilots, making it difficult to fly for those not trained in their ways.

TAIM CO. SDS 8/5 DUAL LASER CANNONS (2): Four emitter muzzles project from the underbelly of the ship and deliver a blistering laser attack.

SIRPLEX J-4 DEFLECTOR GENERATOR: Encloses the fighter in a tightly bonded energy shield from forward and aft projectors.

HULL: Ultra-light alloy protects against energy attacks, though it is susceptible to buzz droids.

HYPERBOOST

Primarily designed for space combat, the Delta-7 did not possess a hyperdrive but was fitted for a Syluire-31 hyperspace docking ring. Once the starfighter was docked inside the ring, its astromech droid computed the proper coordinates and the ring's engines took the fighter into lightspeed.

TECHNICAL SPECIFICATIONS

MANUFACTURER: Kuat Systems Engineering

MODEL: Delta-7 *Aethersprite*

CLASS: Starfighter

WIDTH/HEIGHT/DEPTH: 3.92 m × 1.44 m × 8.0 m

WEAPONRY: Dual twin-barrel laser cannons

SHIELDS: Yes

MAXIMUM SPEED: 5,000 G (space) / 1,260 kph (atmosphere)

HYPERDRIVE: No (requires hyperdrive ring)

LIFE SUPPORT SYSTEMS: Yes

CREW: 1 + astromech droid

CONSUMABLES: None (one week with booster ring)

COST: 180,000 Republic dataries new; 145,000 used

COM-SCAN PROCESSOR: The Jedi installed their own multi-mode sensor system and hyperwave transceiver for encrypted communications through hyperspace relays.

ASTROMECH CIRCUIT: An astronavigation droid is permanently hardwired into the fighter. Later models, like the 7B, offer an expanded hull with room for a full-featured astromech socket.

NOVALDEX J-44 "JETFORCE" SUBLIGHT ENGINES (2): Precursors to Novaldex's "Event Horizon" line used in A-wings, these smaller engines require excessive refueling of the reactant tanks.

LANDING GEAR BAY (3): Opens up to release pads for a safe landing on uneven surfaces.

THRUST NOZZLES (2): Focuses and times engine bursts to match the Jedi pilot's fine control.

A-WING ACES

Many Imperial and First Order pilots admit that the A-wing's speed doesn't concern them as much as the fearless beings who fly them. Given the vessel's finicky controls and powerful sublight engines, A-wing pilots have to be relentless risk-takers willing to exploit the A-wing's strengths to pull off the inconceivable.

PILOTS OF THE REBELLION

The courageous pilots who flew the A-wing in the war against the Galactic Empire gave the fighter its sterling reputation for speed and maneuverability.

ARVEL CRYNYD

A former Z-95 pilot for a Thyferran bacta cartel, Arvel Crynyd possessed hyper-quick reflexes and an uncanny spatial sense that made him right at home in an A-wing. As skilled as Crynyd was as a pilot, he was doubly so as a squadron leader. When the rebels made their assault on the second Death Star, Crynyd rallied Green Squadron to make a direct attack on the Imperial flagship *Executor*. They managed to disable the *Executor*'s shields before its turbolasers struck Crynyd's A-wing. Knowing he was about to die, Crynyd aimed his A-wing at the *Executor*'s bridge. The fiery crash not only eliminated Admiral Piett and the Imperial command staff stationed on the bridge, but also sent the kilometers-long *Executor* on a collision course with the Death Star.

JAKE FARRELL

Jake Farrell quit being an Imperial flight instructor when he realized he was training pilots to be cold-blooded killers. Retirement on hardscrabble Derango 4 couldn't contain his itch to be back in a starfighter, and soon he committed himself to the rebel group Yellow Seven. Flying a customized Tammuz-an Spearhead for their squadron, he became a champion of the craft. At Endor, Farrell flew an A-wing under the call sign "Gold Four" and accompanied the *Millennium Falcon* into the Death Star superstructure.

SILA KOTT

As Red Squadron's Red Three, Sila Kott went head to head with the legions of TIE fighters during the Battle of Endor. Kott perished from enemy fire when she tried to lead two interceptors away from her friends. Her homeworld of Toprawa built a flight school in her name to honor her contribution to freedom in the galaxy.

PILOTS OF THE RESISTANCE

The pilots who strap themselves into the cockpits of Resistance A-wings try to live up to the Rebel Alliance's legends and leave their own mark in the war against the First Order.

TALLIE LINTRA

No one in the Resistance is more talented at handling an A-wing than Tallie Lintra. The young and vivacious pilot from Pippip 3 grew up dusting her father's crops in a beat-up RZ-1, so flying an updated RZ-2 is as natural to her as lacing her boots. Resistance leaders saw her leadership potential and promoted her to command Blue Squadron. During the Resistance's evacuation of the base on D'Qar, she led the A-wing escort covering the assault bombers that attacked the First Order's dreadnought.

A-WING BATTLES

For more than three decades, A-wings have played an essential role in the fight against the oppressive Empire and First Order.

DARK LORD'S PREY

Phoenix Home, the flagship of one of the earliest rebel cells, possessed a small but complete squadron of A-wings. These A-wings had sections of their hulls painted either blue or green and guarded the flagship from Imperial attacks. Sadly, the A-wing's trademark speed and agility proved little defense against a lone TIE Advanced fighter flown by Darth Vader, the Emperor's brutal enforcer. Vader single-handedly bested the A-wings in combat, destroying many of the starfighters, as well as the *Phoenix Home*, in the process.

BATTLE OF ENDOR

When the Alliance fleet gathered again after being scattered by the Imperial attack on their base at Hoth, many of the disparate rebel starfighter squadrons were united. A-wings joined X-wings and Y-wings in an assault on a new Death Star being constructed above the forest moon of Endor. The element of surprise seemed to be in the rebels' favor until the Imperial fleet, led by the Super Star Destroyer *Executor*, emerged from the other side of the moon. For all their speed, the A-wings of Green and Red Squadrons couldn't outmaneuver the overwhelming numbers of TIE fighters and interceptors coming at them. But they never backed down. Along with the destruction of the *Executor*, A-wing squadrons also took down the cruiser *Pride of Tarlandia*, which coordinated Imperial communications.

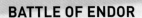

BATTLE OF JAKKU

Nearly five years after the Rebellion's surprise victory at Yavin, the forces of the New Republic clashed against the remnants of the Empire on the isolated world of Jakku. A-wing squadrons were among the many starfighters the New Republic deployed to combat the thousands of TIE fighters launched from Imperial Star Destroyers. Countless A-wings took heavy fire and met an explosive end, crashing in Jakku's desert sands. These sacrifices were not in vain. The New Republic won the battle and drove the Imperials out of the galaxy. Soon afterward, componentry of the crashed A-wings found a second life as scrap tech for Jakku's scavengers.

EVACUATION ESCORT

After Poe Dameron's squadrons destroyed Starkiller Base, the First Order sought out the Resistance headquarters on the planet D'Qar to enact their revenge. A-wings flew guard around the Resistance fleet and the transports fleeing the base. When three First Order warships emerged from hyperspace to attack, a squadron of A-wings, commanded by Tallie Lintra, assisted Poe Dameron and the Resistance's assault bombers in taking on an enemy dreadnought.

A-WINGS THROUGH THE YEARS

Since its breakout appearance in *Return of the Jedi*, the A-wing starfighter has been a mainstay in the *Star Wars* universe. This fan favorite has been featured in television cartoons, video games, toys, books, and even push-button calculators.

MODEL MAKER

MPC introduced the first replica A-wing as a simple, snap-fitting model kit during the opening run of *Return of the Jedi*. The starfighter was produced on a 1:48 scale and contained twenty-two styrene parts, a transparent stand, waterslide decals, and laser cannons that rotated in place. The kit has remained popular with amateur builders and has been reissued multiple times since its release in 1983.

TELEVISION STAR

The A-wing soared through the airwaves as a vessel on the 1985 Saturday-morning cartoon *Star Wars: Droids*, which recounted the early adventures of C-3PO and R2-D2. The craft returned for another animated appearance thirty years later, for 2015's Season Two premiere of *Star Wars Rebels*, when the A-wings of Phoenix Squadron took on the Empire.

TOY JOY

The A-wing didn't make its Kenner toy debut until 1985, when a model ship was packaged under the *Droids* banner. Additionally, an action figure for the green-suited pilot was released as part of the *Droids* and *Star Wars: The Power of the Force* toy waves. Kenner's *Star Wars* line was waning in sales by that time since no new films were on the horizon, and consequently, only a limited number of these toys were produced. Both the ship and figurine became collectibles in the following years.

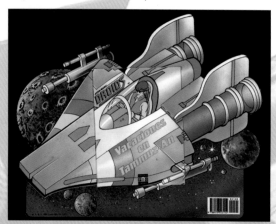

STORIED STARFIGHTER

The A-wing has received a number of differing backstories in *Star Wars* literature over the years. West End Games' 1987 *Star Wars Sourcebook* noted the fighter had been developed since the early days of armed rebellion, yet future supplements mentioned that General Dodonna had ordered it to be built after the Battle of Yavin. This history changed when the A-wings were incorporated into the animated show *Star Wars Rebels*.

GAMER'S DELIGHT

In 1993, LucasArts' best-selling flight simulator *Star Wars: X-Wing* allowed fans to turn their personal computer into the cockpit controls of not only the game's namesake fighter, but also an A-wing. This was the first time players could experience the thrilling speed of an A-wing while dogfighting TIE fighters and avoiding Star Destroyer turbolasers. The A-wing would become a staple of future *Star Wars* video games, including Star Wars: Rogue Squadron and the Star Wars: Battlefront games.

MINIATURE MAYHEM

Galoob Toys introduced *Star Wars* versions of its popular Micro Machines line in 1994. A palm-sized A-wing was sold in a tri-pack with a Y-wing and TIE fighter, while under the "Action Fleet" label, a bigger, four-inch A-wing was available with a pilot "mini-fig." Fantasy Flight Games produced its own micro A-wings in 2014 for its *X-Wing*

Miniatures Game, with one A-wing painted red and another blue. The latter was a homage to the work of legendary *Star Wars* concept designer Ralph McQuarrie, who created a famous piece of concept art for *Return of the Jedi* featuring A-wings with blue decals.

PERSONAL NAVICOMPUTER

For students in need of astronavigational computations, or just help on their mathematics homework, Tiger Electronics issued a solar-powered calculator in the shape of an A-wing in 1997. Sliding open the cockpit revealed a numerical keypad where one could access several different mathematical functions and play three authentic *Star Wars* sound effects. Perhaps this explains why the A-wing lacked an astromech droid: The pilots had their own number crunchers!

BLOCK-BY-BLOCK

LEGO bricklayers of all ages could finally add the A-wing to their block bins in 2013. The A-wing kit was made up of 177 pieces, which, when assembled, formed a seven-inch-long version of the ship, along with a removable engine, four missiles, and three Minifigures: a brow-scrunching A-wing pilot, wise-guy Han Solo, and a fish-eyed Admiral Ackbar.

BEHIND THE SCENES

"Creating new ships comes down to designing something you've never seen before. It has to do with taking the character of the ship and taking the character who is using it and trying to tell a little bit of the story."
—Joe Johnston

NEW ADDITIONS

Return of the Jedi, released in 1983, first introduced the A-wing to the *Star Wars* universe. Concept artist Joe Johnston developed the ship's earliest designs in black marker ink. The new starfighter looked remarkably different from the X-wing or Y-wing and had a wide, trapezoidal shape with perpendicular wing vanes.

WHAT'S IN A NAME

Contrary to the popular belief that the names of the fighters were related to the fact that they were shaped like the letter "A," the model makers originally called the A-wing the "A-fighter" because it was the first of two new starfighter designs featured in the space battle for *Return of the Jedi*. The second craft was subsequently designated the "B-wing."

RACING STRIPES

Ralph McQuarrie's full-color illustration of the A-wings (below) elaborated on Joe Johnston's sketches in striking fashion. Along with painting the shaded region from Johnston's A-wing a bright blue, he also added a white triangle in the front prow for more distinction. When the A-wing was built, the model makers replaced the blue with red, a color that wouldn't disappear when shot against a bluescreen during the filming of the visual effects sequences. More than thirty years later, the animated show *Rebels* would resurrect McQuarrie's paint job for the A-wing fighters of Phoenix Squadron.

R.M'QUARRIE

DON'T MESS WITH SUCCESS

The starship models seen in *Star Wars: A New Hope* and *The Empire Strikes Back* became such icons of popular culture that for *Return of the Jedi* the Model Shop at Industrial Light & Magic (ILM) was trusted to do its job with minimal interference. As a result, some miniatures, like the A-wing, didn't have the detailed blueprints that were more common in the previous films. Model makers relied on their imaginations to find ways to customize and improve on the designs. The model above was built by ILM Model Shop Supervisor Lorne Peterson and Chief Mold Maker Wesley Seeds.

JACKS OF ALL TRADES

The ILM Model Shop was full of people trained in a variety of professions and crafts, from boat building and airplane construction to carpentry, industrial product design, and electronics machining. Model makers had to work with wood, plastics, aluminum, and foam, the core components of miniature building. They also had to be adept at dipping into buckets of store-bought plastic model kits to find accessories (known to the artists as "greebles" and "nurnies") to garnish their models—such as the figurine of the World War I German pilot who was fitted into the A-wing cockpit!

MATH MATTERS

Before building a model like the A-wing, ILM's model makers worked out a formula to determine the model's scale, using reference photos of markers on a miniature set to figure out a constant for measurements. They informed the cameraman of these scales, discovered what kind of lenses would be used, and, if the effects shot showed people in it, deciphered the size of human beings on a physical set. Forgoing the mathematics and merely "eyeballing" scales during the model building often led to mistakes that could cost thousands of dollars and weeks of lost time.

SMALL FRY

The A-wing was the most compact rebel starfighter built for the original *Star Wars* trilogy. Lorne Peterson and Wesley Seeds put together the A-wing from Joe Johnston's sketches and Ralph McQuarrie's painting. Peterson had experience working with the fighter's trapezoidal configuration since it bore a similarity to the shape of snowspeeders in *The Empire Strikes Back*.

SUIT-UP

Artist Nilo Rodis-Jamero originated the A-wing flight suits (right), which were made from a green fabric, in contrast to the orange X-wing suits. An ejection harness with white crash straps was connected to a chest control pack, and the helmet featured an extended microphone and a pull-down blast shield meant to protect the pilot's eyes from bright explosions.

PILOT SWAP

For live-action shots, flesh-and-blood actors—not plastic World War I figurines—played the roles of A-wing pilots. English actress Poppy Hands played Red Three, though the dialogue she recorded on the set was not used. In post-production, a male American actor dubbed her lines. Nonetheless, Red Three is recognized as female in official *Star Wars* lore and was later given the full name Sila Kott.

CANNONBALL RUN

For the scene in *Return of the Jedi* in which an A-wing was hit by turbolaser fire and crashed into the Super Star Destroyer, Joe Johnston's initial storyboards depicted an X-wing and named the kamikaze pilot Mad Maxx (below). When the doomed ship became an A-wing, Rodis-Jamero illustrated the storyboard (bottom) showing its final moments.

COMPOSITE CREATOR

Visual effects artist Ken Ralston was in charge of putting together the action-packed space battle between the Imperial and rebel fleets. For shots that had multiple craft in them, such as A-wings and X-wings dogfighting TIE fighters, each model had to be filmed on its own as a separate element. These elements were then combined onto a single frame through a sophisticated optical printer. The process was complicated and time-consuming, with some shots combining over five hundred pieces of film. But the work paid off, winning Ken Ralston and the team at ILM a Special Achievement in Visual Effects Oscar® at the Academy Awards® in 1984.

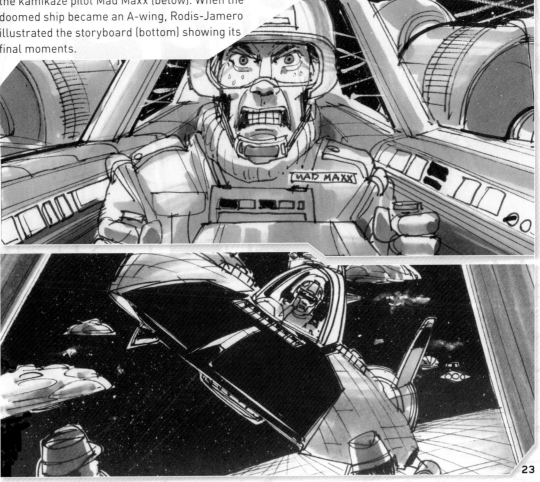

MATTE IT UP

Not all A-wings seen in *Return of the Jedi* were three-dimensional miniatures. The interior shot of the rebel hangar, where three A-wing fighters were parked, was actually a large matte painting by Michael Pangrazio (right). The Automatte motion control camera system, developed for *Jedi*, could shoot flat artwork with an anamorphic lens and permitted actual camera moves within compositions. For the hangar, two ILM staff members were filmed walking across a bare stage and inserted into the center of the shot, bringing live motion to an otherwise static painting.

COMPUTER KITBASHING

For *Star Wars: The Last Jedi*, the drafting of ships like the A-wing began in 3D graphics programs like Rhino and Maya. Designers could pick out various premade elements from a virtual toolbox to add details and "kit-bash" like the original ILM team did by adding pieces of store-bought models. Often, the artists would 3D print the designs so director Rian Johnson could hold them and see how they would look when built physically.

RALPH'S RETURN

Rian Johnson and his team decided to make the A-wing in *The Last Jedi* resemble McQuarrie's rendering of the starfighter in his *Return of the Jedi* concept painting. The new A-wing featured different proportions than the old one, including a slimmer and more streamlined body, in line with what McQuarrie had imagined. Design supervisor Kevin Jenkins created several pieces of A-wing concept art for *The Last Jedi* including a striking illustration depicting the A-wings escorting the Resistance fleet (right).

Kev Jenkins/Space Bar

25

INTERVIEW WITH KEVIN JENKINS

One of the few artists involved in all phases of film production, Kevin Jenkins is responsible for maintaining a singular visual style throughout the *Star Wars* sequel trilogy. He grew up in Southampton, England, and trained as a technical illustrator, creating art for advertisers, computer games, and science fiction book covers for many years before joining the visual effects team behind the BBC's *Walking with Dinosaurs*. In 2013, after working under production designer Rick Carter on director Steven Spielberg's *War Horse* and *Lincoln*, Jenkins began his tenure at Industrial Light & Magic (ILM) as a supervising art director on *The Force Awakens*. He was promoted to design supervisor at Lucasfilm for the next two movies and has contributed designs for many of the vehicles and sets, including the updated A-wing starfighter in *The Last Jedi*.

HOW DID YOU APPROACH CONCEPTUALIZING THE NEW A-WING?

We returned to the inspiration, the DNA of *Star Wars*, which is Ralph McQuarrie. His style, one could say, is the Tudor period, the Elizabethan period, the Art Deco of *Star Wars*. We looked at Ralph's concept painting of the A-wing, and the period stylization was what caught everyone's eye [and we thought], yeah, [we'd] love to see that flying. The A-wing in *Return of the Jedi* is slightly curved and round, but Rian decided to go more retro-futuristic in line with Ralph's original concept art, which is slightly square or slightly more blocky, slightly more '80s.

WHY DID DIRECTOR RIAN JOHNSON CHOOSE THE A-WING?

Talking to each director, we all have our favorite ships from the time period that *Star Wars* influenced us. [Director] J. J. Abrams wanted to update the X-wing for *The Force Awakens*, and so Rian also wanted to update some ships for *The Last Jedi*. It was like, what's your favorite? The A-wing. That was how it was started!

WHAT DIFFERENTIATES THE NEW A-WING FROM ITS PREDECESSOR IN *RETURN OF THE JEDI*?

Slimness. If you look at that Ralph painting with a blue stripe and triangle on it, to be honest with you, it's that to a T. Much like the X-wing from *The Force Awakens* was based upon Ralph's concept painting of the split-wing fighter, the A-wing takes on all those proportions that are in Ralph's painting. The only thing that's different is our paint job. I designed a kind of retro '70s coloring for it and we didn't add the blue triangle, but fundamentally, if you've seen Ralph's painting, you're looking at it. Funnily enough, I don't think there's much concept art on the vehicle because we pretty much prototyped it straightaway as a 3D printed model.

WHAT'S YOUR EXPERIENCE BUILDING MODELS?

I used to build Lancaster bombers as a kid. I'd paint them so badly and get glue stuck on my fingers and the cockpit that I'd get very frustrated. As a slightly older version of myself, I've bought some of those old kits I had made and after being an artist for over thirty years, I think I got a bit better, and I've made some quite nice models. By the end of the physical shoot of *The Force Awakens*, I think there were about thirty-five models set all over my desk in various stages of paint.

DID THIS INFLUENCE THE WAY YOU DESIGNED SHIPS LIKE THE A-WING?

I turned the conceptualization process back into a more uncomputery way of working. That wasn't because I was being romantic or nostalgic, but because the original models were made in a period way and I thought we should make models of the new ships to see what we needed to do. 3D printing allows you to speed up the process enormously. For the fine grain of the models—the noise, the gack, the greebles—I've got boxes and boxes of tank parts all over the floor in the office. I used them to decorate the 3D printed models

as they did in the '70s. With the A-wing, we were building it as we were designing it, then adding gack to it. It was a very immediate process. Filmmaking can be a fast-paced business, and you just have to keep up with the production.

WHAT WAS THE PROCESS OF CONSTRUCTING THE A-WING FOR LIVE-ACTION FILMING?

This was the first time an A-wing was ever built as a physical model prop. We made a red and a blue [version], and they were mostly used on set for the pilots getting up into them, sitting in them, all that kind of stuff. For actual cockpit pilot shots, the A-wings were mounted on the gimbal so the vehicle could rotate. The only major change we made was that we replaced the flat glass canopy from Ralph's beautiful painting with a rounder canopy to eliminate potential reflection problems of shooting the camera in the pilot's face.

WERE THE OTHER A-WINGS ANIMATED DIGITALLY?

We only built a limited amount of in-camera stuff on set. We made two A-wings, but maybe there are six or eight in the film, and the rest obviously are computer-generated iterations. The 3D animated build comes from the physical model, but then if there's any change, normally it's only texturally.

WHAT WOULD YOU DO TO YOUR INCREDIBUILDS™ MODEL TO MAKE IT SPECIAL?

If I was to personalize it, I would put the same paint job on it that Rian approved, which is a lovely blue retro '70s stripe running down the middle of it. The blue was my homage to a Ralph's painting of the two A-wings that influenced me so much as a kid. Rian had the choice of many colors, but of all the concept paint jobs I did, he chose the one that was my nod to Ralph.

INTERVIEW WITH JAMES CLYNE

James Clyne served as senior art director on *Star Wars: The Last Jedi* and collaborated with other artists at Industrial Light & Magic (ILM) on the design for the new A-wing and the assault bomber. Clyne grew up in Oregon, drawing and doodling to his heart's content, then studied fine art at UC Santa Barbara and design at the ArtCenter in Pasadena. During his career in the film industry, he has worked on over thirty motion pictures, including Steven Spielberg's *A.I. Artificial Intelligence* and *Minority Report*, as well as James Cameron's *Avatar* and both of J. J. Abrams's Star Trek movies. In 2013, he joined the preproduction team for *Star Wars: The Force Awakens*.

WHAT WAS YOUR MODEL BUILDING EXPERIENCE AS A KID? DID IT INFLUENCE YOUR ART?

My bedroom looked like it was set-dressed for a Steven Spielberg movie! I had B-52 and F-4 Phantom models hung on fishing wire from the ceiling. When making the models, I was obsessive with the amount of detail and paintwork. What drew me to [work on *Star Wars*] is that *Star Wars* models felt like the same models that I was building as a kid. I was never as talented as the original model makers, but I appreciated the fact that those models looked realistic and weren't brand-new things off the shelf. They looked like

they had seen better days. They had dirt, stains, rust, and all those wonderful things that I think were new to movie-making at the time. You saw these futuristic science-fiction vehicles in a different way, as living, breathing things.

HOW DID YOU GET STARTED ON CONTRIBUTING TO THE DESIGN OF THE NEW *STAR WARS* FILMS?

I was part of the team of concept artists on *The Force Awakens*. We worked with Rick Carter, the production designer, for the first year or so asking questions rather than answering them. There were a lot of questions like: Where are we in the *Star Wars* universe thirty years past *Return of the Jedi*? What does it mean to be a sequel to *Return of the Jedi*? What does the universe look like? How much should these new films feel like the original trilogy? How much should they depart from the originals? The script was still in an infant stage when we started, so we were able to explore a lot. What we found out, going to director J. J. Abrams for advice, was that he was a big fan of episodes IV, V, and VI. So we leaned on those films heavily and pushed some of the classic designs around based on his need for *The Force Awakens* to feel very nostalgic and vintage. J. J.'s favorite ship was the X-wing, so we made sure we had an X-wing in there!

CAN YOU DESCRIBE WORKING WITH *THE LAST JEDI* DIRECTOR RIAN JOHNSON ON THE DESIGNS?

Rian is obviously a huge *Star Wars* fan first and foremost. Knowing where we are in our *Star Wars* timeline after Episode VII, he wanted to make sure that there were still signatures in Episode VIII from Episodes IV, V, and VI and that we didn't just throw out all those old-school ideas. He was great at making sure I stayed on track and distilled a design down to the very basic shapes. When he finally got something to where he liked it, he stuck with it. He wouldn't try twelve different things. He was very consistent that way.

WHAT INFORMS YOUR PROCESS WHEN YOU'RE DESIGNING A SHIP?

I would go back to what George Lucas said early on before Episode IV was made. One: Could an eight-year-old draw it quickly? Two: Is it a memorable silhouette? He drew an X-wing and TIE fighter and Death Star and they're the simplest sketches. Yet in their simplicity is an ability to be memorable. They're just very memorable shapes because they're so simple. But that simplicity is really, for me as a designer, a difficult thing to achieve sometimes.

WHY DID THE A-WING MAKE A REAPPEARANCE IN *THE LAST JEDI*?

The A-wing is a ship that Rian always loved. We hadn't seen it since *Return of the Jedi*, so he wanted it to be a part of his story. He wanted it to be a part of this opening battle that we see in the film. They're little support ships for the bomber. Because I was working on the bomber, we had to make sure that the A-wing and bomber worked together. They had to feel like they were in the same world, not only in color and pattern but

also in shape. I actually did an illustration that showed the A-wing with the bomber. A decision was made to change the A-wing a bit to look like Ralph McQuarrie's original painting of the A-wing, versus what we see in *Return of the Jedi*. Then a lot of effort went into drafting blueprints for full-size construction.

HOW DO YOU THINK THE A-WING COMPARES TO THE OTHER SHIPS?

It's one of the more streamlined ships in the fleet. If you look at the X-wing, for example, it has very faceted planes and more primitive shapes. The A-wing has these compound curves. Some of its sleekness was just its inherent design, but the other part was that the artists and model makers had the ability to do more compound curves and more streamlined shapes by the time they got to film *Return of the Jedi*. In the first *Star Wars* movie, they had to work in primitives because what they had available were simple styrene planes built on primitive shapes. As the movies progressed, the model makers became more advanced in their abilities to do customized shapes. The A-wing to me represents a very slick automotive look for a *Star Wars* ship . . . I always felt the A-wing could have been inspired by the Porsche Spyder, the infamous car that James Dean drove in *Rebel Without a Cause*. The Spyder is very curved with elegant, smooth shapes to it.

WHAT WOULD YOU DO TO CUSTOMIZE YOUR OWN INCREDIBUILDS™ A-WING MODEL?

I like how the A-wing has these big, bold, beautiful colors to it, especially the McQuarrie version. It has a big blue stripe with a white triangle. I would try something as bold and simple as that. I would put a shape on it like an octagon rather than a triangle. There were red A-wings in *Return of the Jedi*, and blue and green ones in *The Last Jedi*, so I'd paint mine yellow or orange.

MAKE IT YOUR OWN

One of the great things about IncrediBuilds™ models is that each one is completely customizable. The untreated natural wood can be decorated with paints, pencils, pens, beads, sequins—the list goes on and on!

Before you start building and decorating your model, choose a theme and make a plan. You can create a replica of the A-wing starfighter, or you can make something completely different. Anything goes! Read through this sample project to get you started and those creative juices flowing.

WHAT YOU NEED:
- Paints (black, white, gray, and blue)
- Paintbrush
- Pencil

WHAT YOU MIGHT WANT:
- Cotton swab
- Black and brown chalk pastel or charcoal

It will be easier to craft the A-wing with the model fully assembled.

STEPS:

1. Paint the entire model gray and let dry.

2. Paint the entire model white over the gray. It's okay for the gray to show through a little to convey wear and tear on the ship.

3. Paint the engraved details: the windows, the blue stripes, etc. Use a pencil for the very small details.

4. Paint thin layers of watered-down black paint to depict the burnt areas at the front of the ship. Use the same watered-down black paint to fill in the darker plates at the back of the ship.

5. Rub a pencil over some areas to show more grime and wear.

6. If you'd like, you can use a cotton swab to dab on brown and black chalk pastel or charcoal until you get the effect you prefer.

SOURCES

Astleford, Gary, Owen K. C. Stephens, and Rodney Thompson. *Starships of the Galaxy.* 2nd ed. Renton, WA: Wizards of the Coast, 2007.

Blackman, Haden. *The New Essential Guide to Vehicles and Vessels.* New York: Del Rey, 2003.

Bouzereau, Laurent. *Star Wars: The Annotated Screenplays.* New York: Del Rey, 1997.

Bray, Adam, Cole Horton, Kerrie Dougherty, and Michael Kogge. *Star Wars: Absolutely Everything You Need to Know.* New York: Dorling Kindersley, 2015.

Bray, Adam. *Star Wars Rebels Visual Guide: Epic Battles.* New York: Dorling Kindersley, 2015.

Build the Millennium Falcon. Issue 29. London: De Agostini UK, 2015.

Catalano, Katherine. "Special Effects." *Bantha Tracks* 21. San Rafael, CA: Official *Star Wars* Fan Club, 1983.

——. "Modelmaking." *Bantha Tracks* 22. San Rafael, CA: Official *Star Wars* Fan Club, 1983.

Dougherty, Kerrie, Curtis Saxton, David West Reynolds, and Ryder Windham. *Star Wars Complete Vehicles.* New York: Dorling Kindersley, 2013.

Johnson, Shane. *Star Wars Technical Journal of the Rebel Forces.* New York: Starlog, 1994.

Kogge, Michael. *Poe Dameron: Flight Log.* White Plains, NY: Studio Fun, 2016.

Murphy, Paul. *The Rebel Alliance Sourcebook.* Honesdale, PA: West End Games, 1990.

Peterson, Lorne. *Sculpting a Galaxy.* San Rafael, CA: Insight Editions, 2006.

Rinzler, J. W. *The Making of Return of the Jedi.* New York: Del Rey, 2013.

——, ed. *Star Wars Storyboards: The Original Trilogy.* New York: Abrams, 2014.

Slavicsek, Bill and Curtis Smith. *The Star Wars Sourcebook.* Honesdale, PA: West End Games, 1987.

Smith, Bill. *The Essential Guide to Vehicles and Vessels.* New York: Del Rey, 1996.

Cover illustration by Ralph McQuarrie

Page 9 image from Star Wars: Battlefront

Images on pages 18–19 are courtesy of RanchoObiWan.org. Rancho Obi-Wan is a nonprofit museum in Northern California that is home to the Guinness World Records' largest collection of *Star Wars* memorabilia, owned by author and collector Steve Sansweet. For information about membership and tours, go to RanchoObiWan.org.

Insight Editions, in association with Roots of Peace, will plant two trees for each tree used in the manufacturing of this book. Roots of Peace is an internationally renowned humanitarian organization dedicated to eradicating land mines worldwide and converting war-torn lands into productive farms and wildlife habitats. Roots of Peace will plant two million fruit and nut trees in Afghanistan and provide farmers there with the skills and support necessary for sustainable land use.

MANUFACTURED IN CHINA

10 9 8 7 6 5 4 3 2 1

IncrediBuilds™
A Division of Insight Editions, LP
PO Box 3088
San Rafael, CA 94912
www.insighteditions.com
www.incredibuilds.com

Find us on Facebook: www.facebook.com/InsightEditions
Follow us on Twitter: @insighteditions

Library of Congress Cataloging-in-Publication Data available.

ISBN: 978-1-68298-095-8

Publisher: Raoul Goff
Associate Publisher: Jon Goodspeed
Art Director: Chrissy Kwasnik
Designers: Yousef Ghorbani and Alison Corn
Senior Editor: Chris Prince
Managing Editor: Alan Kaplan
Editorial Assistant: Holly Fisher
Production Editor: Carly Chillmon
Associate Production Manager: Sam Taylor
Product Development Manager: Rebekah Piatte
Model Designer: Ryan Zhang, TeamGreen
Craft Sample: Steve Kongsle

For Lucasfilm:
Assistant Editor: Samantha Holland
Senior Editor: Frank Parisi
Creative Director of Publishing: Michael Siglain
Art Director: Troy Alders
Story Group: James Waugh, Pablo Hidalgo, and Leland Chee
Image Unit: Steve Newman, Newell Todd, Gabrielle Levenson, Erik Sanchez, Bryce Pinkos, Tim Mapp, and Nicole Lacoursiere